COLIN POWELL

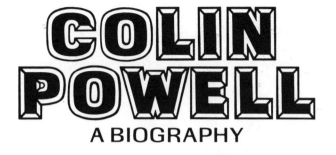

A BIOGRAPHY

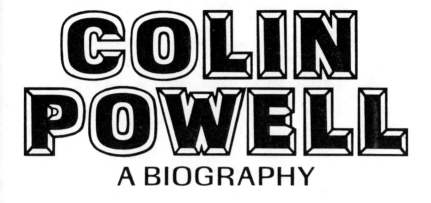

A BIOGRAPHY

JIM HASKINS

SCHOLASTIC INC.
New York Toronto London Auckland Sydney

PHOTO CREDITS

Cover: © 95 Cindy Karp, *Black Star*.

pp. 8, 10, 14, 17, 23, 27, 30, 33, 38, Powell Family photos; p. 18, The City College of New York/CUNY; p. 2, The Office of the Chairman, The Joint Chiefs of Staff; p. 41, The Special Collections Division, U.S.M.A. Library, West Point, New York; p. 44, The U.S. Navy; pp. 46, 49, 54, 58, 66, 69, 72, 75, 78, 81, 83, 85, 90, AP/Wide World; p. 62, Johnny Crawford; p. 87, Sara Krucwich, *The New York Times*; p. 93, The Morris High School Alumni Association.

ISBN 0-590-89815-9

12 11 10 9 8 7 6 5 4 3 2 1   4   6 7 8 9/9 0 1/0

Printed in the U.S.A.   40

To Alfred

Acknowledgments

I am grateful to General Colin Powell and his office for their help. Thanks also to Ann Kalkhoff, Ann Jefferies, and Kathy Benson.

Contents

COLIN POWELL

A BIOGRAPHY

The official photo of General Colin Powell, Chairman of the Joint Chiefs of Staff.

1
Boyhood in the Bronx

I grew up in a time of wars," says General Colin Powell. "My earliest memories are of World War II. I was four years old when that war started."

Like most other little boys growing up at that time, Colin played war on the streets of the South Bronx neighborhood where his family lived. He carried a homemade bayonet and pretended to invade enemy territory. He studied pictures of his older cousin James Lopez Watson, who was serving in the U.S. Army in Italy, and imagined being a brave soldier in a faraway place. But Colin didn't really know what that war, or war itself, was all about.

As he grew up, Colin came to understand that war is the way peoples and nations settle their differences when they cannot or will not use other solutions. As a college student, he would prepare for war, but nothing prepared him for the first one in which he served — the undeclared war in Vietnam. He learned from the Korean and later the Vietnam conflicts that a nation can make war without declaring war.

Colin Powell then lived through the Cold War, when there was a constant threat of real war between the United States and its allies and the Soviet Union and its allies. And just when that Cold War ended after some forty years, and some people were talking about the possibility of a lasting peace, Powell was one of the key men who planned a major United States-led campaign in the Middle East.

Other American men have had experiences similar to Colin Powell's. But Powell is the first black man to serve in the highest military position in the United States. As the first black and the youngest Chairman of the Joint Chiefs of Staff, he has been the most visible man to hold that position in the history of the United States. As the man who oversaw the first declared war to which the United States had been committed since World War II, the rescue of the nation of Kuwait, he was a black military hero whom all Americans could admire.

Colin Luther Powell was born on April 5, 1937, in Harlem, in New York City. It was the time of the Great Depression. Many people had no jobs, and the entire nation was suffering through serious financial problems. These problems were especially severe in the largely black section of Harlem. Because of racial discrimination, African-

Americans had been the first to lose their jobs, and since many were barely making ends meet to begin with, it did not take them long to sink into terrible poverty. People stood for hours in long lines to get free bread and soup. Many could not pay their rent and were evicted from their apartments.

Young Colin's family was luckier than many other families in Harlem. They had a place to live and food to eat. Colin's father had a steady job as a shipping clerk in the garment district downtown. (He later became a foreman of a garment factory.) Other relatives worked in the printing trades. Colin's parents were hardworking people who were determined to make a good life for their children, five-and-a-half-year-old Marilyn and the baby Colin.

Both Luther Theophilus Powell and Maud Ariel Powell had moved to New York from the area of Christiana on the British island of Jamaica in the 1920s. Maud Powell had come to join her mother, who had arrived earlier by way of Panama and Cuba. When Maud left Jamaica, she left behind four sisters and three brothers. In New York they moved in with relatives or close friends and became part of a large extended family where everyone was an aunt or an uncle or a cousin.

Both Luther and Maud Powell had attended high school in Jamaica, although only Maud had graduated. Both had benefited from their rigorous British schooling and believed firmly in education as the key to success. Both had attended the Anglican Church in Jamaica and were High

Episcopalians in the United States. The High Episcopalian Church stresses ritual and is similar in many respects to the Roman Catholic Church. The Powells regarded themselves as British subjects and were proud to be, right up to the time they became American citizens.

Colin was given his father's first name as his own middle name. His parents used the British pronunciation KAH-lin. He was too young to remember the Great Depression. His earliest memories of the larger world around him were of World War II, the conflict that raged first in Europe and then in the Pacific. He was four years old when the Japanese bombed the U.S. naval base at Pearl Harbor, Hawaii, and the United States entered the war on both the Pacific and European fronts. His parents always read the daily newspapers and discussed current events, and Colin had some sense of how important the fight was to "keep the world safe for democracy." The words *army* and *navy* were part of his vocabulary at a very early age.

So was the name of an American hero in the war, Captain Colin P. Kelly, who was killed bombing a Japanese warship. Captain Kelly's first name was pronounced KOH-lin. Colin Powell recalls, "My friends in the streets of the South Bronx, who heard Captain Kelly's name pronounced on the radio, by their parents, and other adults, began to refer to me by the same pronunciation. So, I grew up with my friends saying KOH-lin and my family saying KAH-lin." Today General Powell uses the American pronunciation.

His first memories of where he lived are of the apartment on Kelly Street in the Hunts Point section of the South Bronx, where his family moved when he was about three. Today the South Bronx is regarded as a terrible slum, and Powell's old neighborhood (the site of his old apartment building is now a parking lot) is the drug- and crime-infested 41st Police Precinct, nicknamed "Fort Apache." But in the 1940s, moving there was a step up for the Powell family. They found a four-bedroom apartment in a building at 952 Kelly Street, which they shared at times with Colin's grandmother and various aunts. The other tenants were mostly Jewish, recently arrived immigrants from Europe. From them and their children, young Colin picked up words in Yiddish that he would later find quite useful. The neighborhood was mixed, with Hispanics and a few other black families. It was a safe neighborhood, where everyone looked out for one another, and if a kid got into mischief, he suddenly found himself with about twenty "parents" scolding him.

Colin Powell says that when he was growing up, he did not realize he was a "minority": "I didn't know I was a minority because everybody there was a minority. Ours was a neighborhood of young blacks and Puerto Ricans, mixed with a large Jewish population. . . . We all lived in each other's homes, and our parents all knew each other. Peo-

Powell with neighborhood pals on Kelly Street. Left to right: Victor Ramirez, Anthony Grant, Powell, and Edward Grabliauskas.

ple got along, even though you never lost your cultural identity. It wasn't a real melting pot, but we could kid each other. The usual epithets were thrown back and forth."

"The world was mine," he remembers happily. "I had a close family, which provided everything I needed as a kid. And I had freedom in New York City, being able to get on a subway or trolley car and go anywhere I wanted."

Most of the boys in the neighborhood were older than Colin, and since he was not an aggressive boy, he did not get involved in their rough games. He was content to play stickball and soldier, to build things with materials he found in the street or around the house, or to race bicycles with his best friend, Eugene "Gene" Norman. He also spent a lot of time with his large extended family.

He could not have had better influences. Gene grew up to become a successful businessman and the president of the Harlem International Trade Center. Colin's entire family shared the values of hard work and being the best you could be. Altogether, fourteen of the children would go on to earn college degrees.

One of Colin's cousins, J. Bruce Llewellyn, owns Coca-Cola bottling plants and cable television stations. James Lopez Watson, the cousin who served in the Army in Italy in World War II, later became a senior judge on the United States Customs Court of International Trade. James's sister, Barbara Watson, was the United States Ambassador to Malaysia in 1980–1981 and as of this writing is an Assistant Secretary of State in charge of passports. Other cousins became aerospace engineers, college professors, biochemists, teachers, and one became a New York State Supreme Court judge.

Not only was Colin surrounded by ambitious people at home, he was also surrounded by them at school. Colin attended elementary school at P.S. 39 (now P.S. 72) in the Bronx. Its student body was largely Jewish. The children of immigrant parents, Colin's classmates were expected to do well in school, and although Colin's parents also placed great value in education, Colin was by comparison an indifferent student.

At home he was surrounded by books and news-

The Powell family at Marilyn's college graduation, Buffalo, New York, 1952. Left to right: Luther (father), Marilyn (sister), Maud (mother), and Colin.

10

papers, but he just wasn't interested in studying, and he didn't try very hard. His sister, Marilyn, was the one who was always asking their mother to read street signs to her and spell out words when the family went out for a walk. Colin could not have cared less. He was much more likely to ask how something worked, or to find out for himself. He was very interested in mechanical things, in taking things apart and putting them back together. He especially loved cars, but he was good with his hands in many areas and was the family repairman.

Unfortunately, P.S. 39 did not place a high premium on mechanical ability. Students at the school were put into classes according to how well or poorly they did in their studies, and in fifth grade Colin was placed in the "slow," or bottom, class.

That didn't seem to bother Colin. At a young age, he had learned from his parents that the most important thing was to feel good about yourself and not to judge yourself by other people's standards. Luther and Maud Powell wished that their son would work harder in school, because they also believed in hard work. But he was a good son — even-tempered and pleasant, with a good head on his shoulders — and so they found it difficult to be stern with him over his lack of interest in school. As long as he promised to do well enough to pass, and to get into college so he could then get a good job, they were satisfied.

By the time he was a teenager, Colin was regarded by the rest of the family as steady and levelheaded, one who set a good example for his younger cousins. He was an altar boy at St. Margaret's Episcopal Church on 151st Street. But he was not very motivated. His sister, Marilyn, remembers that "he was a pretty average kid."

His cousin Victor remembers looking up to Colin as the elder brother he did not have. But Victor also remembers that when he was about four years old, Colin's mother got so angry when Colin was still in bed by late morning one Saturday that she told little Victor to pour a glass of water over his teenage cousin's head to wake him up. Colin's parents would not tolerate him "wasting himself" by not trying to be somebody. They did not expect him to be a star at anything, but they did expect him to try very hard to get a good job and make something of his life.

Except for lapses like sometimes sleeping late, Colin really did try not to make his parents despair of him. He realized they were working hard for him. His mother, a seamstress, had gone back to work in the garment center once Colin had started school. His father was now a factory foreman in the garment center. Colin saw both of his parents go off to work each weekday morning and come home tired at night. He saw how they made sure that weekends were times for family togetherness. Work and family, work and family — those were the values he learned from the example of his parents. Says Colin, "Somehow, over time, they made it clear to all of us, my sister and myself as well as the extended family of cousins, that there were certain expectations built into the family system."

When Colin entered Morris High School, he was still not very interested in studying. He was a C student throughout the four years, and his parents gave up hope of his transferring to the prestigious public high school, Bronx High School of Science, which some of his older cousins had attended. He was well liked, and when there was something he enjoyed doing, like running track, he pursued his goals of making the track team and winning at meets with great intensity. He had no special career goals. But in spite of liking to sleep late on weekends, he was a hard worker, and he was old enough by now to use his mechanical skills to earn pocket money. He got an after-school job at a local children's furniture store around the corner on Westchester Avenue, fixing carriages and cribs.

By this time Colin had become aware of drugs. The streets of his South Bronx neighborhood were mostly quiet and safe, and Colin had no trouble with gangs or criminals. But there was a corner at the end of Kelly Street where drug dealers hung out. The drugs they sold were mostly heroin and marijuana, and Colin didn't know much about them except what they did to people. He saw addicts nodding on street corners; he heard about deaths from drug overdoses and arrests for drug use. He saw how kids who did not have strong family support got sucked into the drug world. He didn't even think about trying drugs himself. Drug use would not have been tolerated in his family.

Powell at age 18, standing in front of a neighbor's house on Kelly Street, the Bronx, New York.

On graduating from Morris High School in 1954, Colin turned his attention to college. His parents expected him to go. They knew, considering that he was a C student, that he was not going to be a doctor or a lawyer, or a teacher, like his older sister, Marilyn. But they felt that a college degree would give him a much better chance to get a good job, perhaps in the civil service, working for the City of New York. Colin realized they were right. He also wanted to please his parents and show them he appreciated the sacrifices they had made for him. As he said years later, "You realized that these modestly educated immigrants were not doing all this for themselves; they were doing all this for you. So it was unthinkable in the family not to do something. Doing it didn't mean becoming a brain surgeon. It just meant getting educated, getting a job, and going as far as you could with that job."

Colin applied to New York University and was accepted. Even though his grades were not high, the university was looking for minority applicants, and Colin had very high recommendations from his teachers concerning his character. But the $750 tuition at NYU was too much for the Powells to afford. Instead, Colin enrolled at the City College of the City University of New York, where the tuition was only $10.

Among the student body of City College there was much intellectual talk of world and national events. Coming from a family that read the newspaper every day, Colin was able to hold his own in such discussions. But he still was not much of a student. He took the required courses in the first two years. During the second semester of his sophomore year, when he had to choose a major, he decided on geology, because he found it easy.

Also during that semester he decided to join the Army Reserve Officers Training Corps (ROTC) at City College. However, he did not join because he had plans for a military career. Instead, he says, he joined because he liked the uniforms. He had noticed the ROTC cadets hanging around Amsterdam and Convent Avenues near City College, and it seemed to him that they were like a club or fraternity. He also noticed that the girls seemed to like the cadets. There were a few black cadets, and Colin would not be the first black student to join. So, he joined ROTC because he could wear a uniform and because he liked girls. Once he was in ROTC, he pledged to the Pershing Rifles, a precision drill team, because he liked the whipped cords that members wore on their shoulders.

Colin soon found, however, that he was very good at the things stressed in ROTC. "It had to do with the guys around me," he says, "the sense of order that the military brought to my life. When you find something you're good at, you tend to pursue it. I was good at ROTC and not good at physics, calculus, languages . . ." While he got C's in his other subjects, he got A's in all his ROTC courses.

Part of being in ROTC was taking military training in the summer. Colin took his training at Fort

Powell in uniform as Commander of the Guard, ROTC Summer Camp, Fort Bragg, North Carolina, July 1957.

Bragg, North Carolina, and it was there that he was first exposed to racial tension.

It was the mid-1950s, and the civil rights movement had not yet begun. In Washington, D.C., the United States Supreme Court had ruled that "separate but equal" schools were unconstitutional. In Montgomery, Alabama, Rosa Parks had been arrested for refusing to give up her bus seat to a white man, and blacks in Montgomery had stayed off the buses in protest, until the Supreme Court ruled that segregated seating on public transportation was unconstitutional. These events, however, had not had any real effect on the day-to-day life of the South.

Powell saw "Colored" and "White" signs at drinking fountains for the first time. He saw that white officers and black officers had separate officers' clubs. He learned that black soldiers were not looked upon kindly by the white community surrounding Fort Bragg. As a Northerner unused to segregation, Powell could have protested. But he was aware that as a member of the ROTC, he represented the military, and he believed it was not his place to do so. He did believe it was his duty to act professionally, and that is the way he behaved.

Colin's yearbook picture from City College, Class of 1958.

Powell matured in ROTC, and his parents were pleased that he had at last found something he wanted to pursue in earnest. They still despaired of his lack of interest in his studies, and they were worried that he might not graduate from college. But ROTC, and his parents, meant enough to Powell to make him study hard enough to graduate. It took him an extra semester to do so, but he finally received his degree in geology.

At the same time, he graduated at the top of his class in ROTC and was commissioned a second lieutenant in the U.S. Army Infantry. With pay of $60 a week, it wasn't exactly the kind of job his parents had in mind for him. At that time the military services were drafting men, not waiting for them to volunteer. Powell's parents figured he might be drafted anyway, so why shouldn't he serve a couple of years, then get an honorable discharge, and go out and get a real job?

2
Vietnam

By the time Powell entered the Regular Army, conditions for blacks there and in the other branches of the military were better than they had ever been before. Blacks had served in every major war, including the Revolution. They had fought bravely and died for their country, but they had always been treated as second-class soldiers. They had been paid less, consigned to the most menial jobs, and been forced to serve in segregated units, usually under white officers. By World War II, a few black officers had been allowed to command the more than 1,000,000 black troops. Also during that war, blacks had been allowed to train and fly as pilots for the first time. But it wasn't until after World War II that the military services were integrated.

On July 16, 1948, President Harry S. Truman had

issued Executive Order 9981 directing "equality of treatment and opportunity" in the armed forces. Ten years later, when Powell joined the Army, the military was not a racial paradise, but it was much better than before. And, it was more integrated than the rest of American society.

Colin Powell's first posting was to West Germany, where the United States had a large number of soldiers on several bases. After the end of World War II, the Soviet Union had moved to take over more and more territory in Eastern Europe, and the United States had committed itself to protecting Western Europe from the Soviet threat. The possibility of war seemed very real, and Second Lieutenant Colin Powell made it his business to prepare the forty men under his command for anything that might happen. As a brand-new officer, he realized that the men would be testing him, and he concentrated on proving his leadership ability. But from the first, he did not set out to make his men afraid of him. Instead, he believed his job was to take care of them. They responded well to his fairness and his obvious caring. He was a popular officer, and he was able to have fun as well as do his job in West Germany. He enjoyed his first experience in a foreign country.

Still, he was glad to be transferred back to the United States in 1960. He had missed seeing his family. His new posting was to Fort Devens, Massachusetts, and it was easy to make the trip to New York on weekends. By the time he returned to the United States, Colin Powell had decided to make his career in the military, and his family was pleased that he had found something to which he could commit himself.

Not long after he made that decision, Powell made another commitment, this time to a young woman. He met Alma Vivian Johnson on a blind date, and it was love at first sight for both of them. Alma was attending school in Boston. (She holds a master's degree in speech pathology and audiology.) She was the daughter of a high school principal in Birmingham, Alabama, and from a highly respected family. Colin and Alma were married on August 24, 1962, and moved into one of the apartments for married couples on the base. Four months later, Powell was shipped out to Vietnam.

His family in New York was shocked. They had never heard of Vietnam. They had to look it up on a map.

Vietnam, in Southeast Asia, was half a world away from the United States, but some U.S. officials thought there was a Communist threat there and in the other Southeast Asian countries of Laos and Cambodia. Vietnam has been divided into North and South Vietnam in 1954. North Vietnam was Communist. South Vietnam was pro-Western. The United States was sending military advisers to President Ngo Dinh Diem of South Vietnam. Powell, in 1962, was among those advisers.

Powell did not want to leave his new wife, but as a soldier he had to put his duty first. At any rate, he was excited about going. He was twenty-

Snapshot of Captain Colin Powell and two other officers during Powell's first tour in Vietnam, December 1962–November 1963.

four years old and had been training for battle since he was in college. He wanted to see some action.

He traveled to Fort Benning, Georgia, for preliminary training, leaving Alma behind. He believed Alma was strong enough to get along without him. But when he learned that she was expecting a child, part of him wished he did not have to go so far away.

It was very difficult for Powell to be out in the jungles of Vietnam when their first child, a son, Michael, was born. In fact, he was so far out of communication that he did not learn about the event until two weeks later. It was also hard for

Alma to give birth without having her husband with her, but she was a military wife and knew she had to cope alone. When she had learned she was expecting a child, she had gone home to Birmingham, Alabama, to stay with her parents.

The American advisers did not just sit in an office in Saigon, South Vietnam's capital, and give out advice to the South Vietnamese military. They visited the battlefields, checked supply lines, and patrolled near the front lines. Powell was assigned to a South Vietnamese infantry battalion patrolling the border with Laos. While marching through a rice paddy one day in 1963, he stepped into a North Vietnamese trap. It was made of razor-sharp bamboo sticks buried in the ground with the points sticking up just below the surface of the water. The bamboo sticks were meant to do serious injury to whomever stepped on them. One of the sticks pierced Powell's foot. He was sent to a nearby field hospital for treatment and was back on patrol in a few weeks. For his bravery and patrolling so close to enemy territory, he received the Purple Heart, the military's honor for soldiers wounded in action, as well as the Bronze Star.

While Powell was in Vietnam, the civil rights movement in the United States went into full swing. After a series of sit-ins at lunch counters in 1960 by Southern black college students, groups across the South had organized to demonstrate against segregation. In the summer of 1963, the Southern Christian Leadership Conference, whose leader was Dr. Martin Luther King, Jr., had decided to stage a campaign in Birmingham, Alabama. The police reacted with great violence against the demonstrators. They herded them with electrified cattle prods into holding pens for mass arrests and turned police dogs and powerful fire hoses onto peaceful demonstrators. A black church was bombed, killing four young girls.

Powell had been too far away from normal communications to hear exactly what was happening. But when he got home in late 1963 he was shocked and shaken by what might have happened to his young family. He was furious when he found out that his father-in-law had been forced to guard the house with a shotgun, while he himself was in Southeast Asia working in support of the policies of his country.

While his military duties prevented him from actively participating in the civil rights movement, Powell followed it closely in newspapers and on television. He was a great admirer of Dr. Martin Luther King, Jr.: "Abraham Lincoln freed the slaves," he explains, "but it was Martin Luther King who freed the whites, who freed the American people. The real civil war was fought in the 1960s — as important as the battles fought in the 1860s — to free America from segregation one hundred years after freeing the slaves."

Powell's next posting was to Fort Benning, Georgia. He found he could pursue his hobby of fixing up old Volvos at Fort Benning, which he enjoyed.

But in the Deep South, Powell again felt the sting of racism. Alma had not yet joined him with their young son, Michael, and Powell was out looking for a house in the area of Columbus, Georgia, when he stopped at a restaurant to get a hamburger. The waitress asked him if he was an African student. Powell said no. She then asked him if he was Puerto Rican. Again Powell said no. "You're Negro?" she finally said. When Powell said yes, she said, "Well, I can't bring out a hamburger. You'll have to go to the back door."

While Powell can joke about that incident now, at the time it made him furious. There he was, just back from Southeast Asia, serving his country, and he couldn't even sit down and be served a hamburger.

Especially off the base Powell had to be careful not to appear "uppity," as blacks from the North were regarded by local whites. One day Powell was rushing to get back to the base and was driving through Sylacauga, Alabama, at seventy miles an hour. He was driving a German Volkswagen with New York license plates and a bumper sticker that said, "All the Way with LBJ," in support of the election campaign of President Lyndon B. Johnson. He was stopped by a white state policeman who was giving out bumper stickers for Republican candidate Senator Barry Goldwater. Powell recalled that the sheriff "looked at me, the German car, the New York license plate, and the LBJ slogan. There was a moment of suspense. He finally said, 'Boy, get out of here. You are not smart enough to hang around.' "

Life at Fort Benning reflected life in the surrounding area. Like most Southern bases, Fort Benning had been slow to integrate. There was a separate officers' club for blacks, and some white officers openly showed that they didn't think the blacks measured up.

By the time he returned from his tour of duty in Vietnam, Powell had decided that he wanted to rise as high as he could in the Army. That meant getting more schooling, and he decided to enroll in the Army Command and General Staff College

Snapshot of Captain Powell with flag, first tour in Vietnam, December 1962–November 1963.

at Fort Leavenworth, Kansas. He regarded this as a step to attending graduate school, but when he mentioned his plans to the commanding officer, the officer told him, "Your college record isn't good enough."

That made Powell angry. He didn't see what his record at City College had to do with his military career. At City College, he had not known what he wanted to do with his life. Besides, he had graduated at the top of his ROTC class. Fortunately, others in the military were willing to give him a chance. When Powell was accepted into the General Staff College, he was determined to show the commanding officer that he was wrong, by studying as hard as he could. Still, part of him was afraid that his commanding officer might be right. As he told the students at Morris High School in April 1991, "I remember the feeling that you can't make it."

One of the subjects Powell took was military history, and he came to enjoy reading about the great campaigns of the past. But he also worked hard on subjects he did not enjoy as much, and he finished second in his class of 1,244 men. The newspaper *Army Times* carried an article about the top five students in the class. When the commander of Powell's division saw the article, he ordered Powell transferred to headquarters, where the brightest and most promising young officers were assigned.

Meanwhile, Colin and Alma Powell had a second child, a daughter, Linda. When he was called for a second tour in Vietnam, in 1968, it was even harder for him to leave his family and to put his plans for attending graduate school on hold. But once again, he looked forward to being where the action was.

By the time he returned to Vietnam, the United States was deeply involved there, with thousands of troops. However, the United States had not officially declared war on North Vietnam. On the home front, a strong antiwar movement had developed. Powell was aware that it was a very unpopular war, but he was a trained soldier, and if his country needed him, then he was ready to serve.

During his second tour of duty in Vietnam, Powell was the operations officer of his division. He and the division commander and a few aides wanted to see a particular operation, so they took a helicopter. They flew over a very mountainous area, and the landing strip on which they were supposed to set down was very narrow. The pilot was having trouble landing when suddenly one of the blades hit a tree and stopped rotating. The helicopter fell to the ground like a rock.

Powell remembers, "When we crashed, I didn't think about anything but leaving. I hit the belt [unfastened his seat belt], jumped out, and ran a few feet. Then I turned around and realized the helicopter was starting to smoke while men were still in there. I ran back . . ."

Others had escaped, too, and they also went back. The division commander had a fractured

The rubble from the helicopter crash in Vietnam where Powell rescued fellow soldiers and received the Bronze Star and a Soldier's Medal.

shoulder and a concussion, and he was barely conscious. Powell and the others pulled him to safety. Then Powell went back to get another man who had been sitting in the middle of the front seats. The helicopter engine and transmission had shoved his head into the radio. When Powell unbuckled the man's seat belt, he wasn't sure he was alive. Then the man moaned. With the help of other survivors, Powell got the man out and pulled off his helmet. It was bent out of shape, but it had saved his life.

Altogether, Powell made four trips back to the smoking helicopter. He says now that he did not think about danger to himself. Instincts, values, and training came into play as he saved the lives of his fellow soldiers.

"All those make you do it," he says. "Nothing's conscious. And I wasn't alone. Others were doing it. It wasn't anything too heroic."

But the Army considered it so. For his heroism, Powell was awarded the Bronze Star and a Soldier's Medal, bringing to a total of eleven the medals and decorations he won in Vietnam.

Back in the United States after a year in Vietnam, Powell saw firsthand how unpopular the war had become. On college campuses across the nation, students were taking over administration buildings, boycotting classes, and demonstrating against Powell's beloved ROTC to protest the war. At Selective Service System offices, young men were burning their draft cards. Other young men were fleeing to Canada to avoid being drafted into the Army. President Lyndon B. Johnson, a Democrat, had decided not to run for reelection because he knew too many people blamed him for the unending war. At the Democratic National Convention in Chicago in August 1968, antiwar protesters had disrupted the convention. Chicago police had put down the demonstrations brutally. Republican Richard Nixon won the presidency in the election of November 1968, but at first he, too, pursued the war in Vietnam.

The antiwar movement grew stronger, especially after four students protesting the war on the campus of Kent State University in Ohio were gunned down by Ohio National Guardsmen in

1970. By 1971, the movement against the war had ceased to be primarily a youth movement. At a mass rally that year in Washington, D.C., not a single speaker against the war was under thirty. The following year a group of congressmen and senators assembled outside the Capitol to vent their frustration at not being able to do anything inside the halls of Congress to stop a war that still wasn't officially declared.

Finally, real progress began to be made. All sides sent representatives to peace talks in Paris, and in 1973, President Nixon ordered the gradual withdrawal of U.S. forces from Vietnam. The last units left Saigon in 1975.

That period of the late 1960s and early 1970s was one of the lowest points in American history. The war had divided the nation, and there was lingering bitterness on both sides. Many believed the United States had lost its superpower status forever. The military, especially the Army, suffered not only many casualties in Vietnam but also a loss of face that would take years to recover. Returning soldiers were not welcomed home as they had been after World War II. Some Americans blamed them for being in the war; other Americans were embarrassed because they had not won the war. Instead of being proud, many of the soldiers were ashamed of their part in it.

Powell had generally kept his feelings about the Vietnam War to himself, but in April 1990, he made a few statements to Ken Adelman of *The Washingtonian*. He remarked that when you commit armed forces, you'd better have clear political objectives. Adelman reminded him that the objective was to keep South Vietnam free from Communism.

"Okay," said Powell, "you say that now. But we can debate whether we had a clear political objective during the thirteen years of the war. Once you have a clear political objective, you have to make sure that the military can achieve that political objective, that the nation commits enough resources to do the job. Then they must give the commanders enough flexibility to achieve their

Major Colin Powell, second tour in Vietnam, June 1968–July 1969.

goals. In Vietnam, it didn't work out that way. We always have to remember that the American people are not patient. They like quick results."

Powell believes the United States should either have gone into Vietnam to win or stayed out. The United States strategy seemed to be to hold the line but not to do anything drastic. But Powell does not believe in refighting the war. He does not go to see the many movies about the war. He feels compassion for those veterans who still carry emotional scars and who have not been able to put the Vietnam experience behind them.

"I went as a professional soldier," he says. "I served twice as a professional soldier. I didn't have anything like the trauma that an infantryman, the draftee private in the front lines for six months, had. I was an officer."

But he felt bad about what the war, and popular feeling against it, had done to the Army. More than the other branches of the military, the Army seemed to be associated in the American mind with the unpopular war. It would take many years before the United States Army would regain its pride.

Yet Powell believed, and continues to believe, that service in the Army is one of the best experiences a person can have. He knew it had been good for him and felt that, as a black, he'd encountered less discrimination in the Army than he would have had in many areas of civilian life. But he thought it was good for all Americans. "We provide one heck of a social service to this country," he told the interviewer for *The Washingtonian*. "We take in a couple hundred thousand kids a year who generally hope to better themselves, to receive some education, to put some money aside, to reap benefits so they can go to college.

"Two, three, or four years later, we discharge most of them back into American society. They are then much more responsible. They have a better sense of order in their lives, of self-discipline and self-appreciation."

3
In the Power Center

Powell returned to his plan to go to graduate school. Taking advantage of Army opportunities to get a graduate degree while in the service, he enrolled at George Washington University and studied hard. At the same time he was taking care of his family, which by 1970 included a second daughter, Annemarie. While he was always busy, he made sure he took time for his family. His daughter Linda says he never sacrificed his family to his career: "We never felt that his work was more important than we were."

In 1971, after two years of study, he earned his master's degree in business adminstration. He was thirty-five years old, which was much older than most students who earn master's degrees. But it had not bothered him to be older than most of his classmates. He had a very clear path in mind. He had chosen that course of study because he felt it would help him become a better leader. He hoped one day to become a base commander or have some other high-level job. It had not occurred to him to seek work at the highest levels of the military — at the Pentagon in Washington, D.C. — until he received a call from an Army personnel man. The Infantry Branch wanted one of its people to become a White House Fellow. The man suggested that Powell apply.

Powell, who was now a major, applied for a White House fellowship. White House Fellows work as special assistants in various government departments. Powell was chosen as one of seventeen White House Fellows out of 1,500 military and civilian applicants. He was assigned to the Office of Management and Budget.

He went from being an anonymous good soldier to being at the center of power at the White House. During his year-long fellowship he became close friends with Caspar W. Weinberger, Director of the Office of Management and Budget, and with Frank Carlucci, the Assistant Director. He was especially close to Carlucci, from whom he learned the ins and outs of government.

After that year as a White House Fellow, Powell, who was by now a lieutenant colonel, returned to military duty. In 1973, he served as a battalion commander in South Korea, sent specifically to straighten out the 1st Battalion, 32nd Infantry, a unit beset by racial problems and drugs. He later explained how he cleaned up the unit and got the

Above, Lieutenant Colonel Powell in South Korea. Below, Lieutenant Colonel Powell with company commanders in Korea, September 1973–September 1974.

black soldiers and the white soldiers working together: "I threw the bums out of the Army. The rest, we ran four miles every morning, and by night they were too tired to get into any trouble."

The following year, he was rotated home to a staff job at the Pentagon.

In 1975, he enrolled at the National War College. He had completed seven of the nine months of study when he was called on to command the Second Brigade of the 101st Airborne Division at Fort Campbell, Kentucky. In spite of having missed the last two months of his studies at the National War College, he graduated with distinction in 1976.

In that year, Jimmy Carter of Georgia, a Democrat, was elected President of the United States, and the following year Powell was promoted to full colonel and made chief military aide to the Special Assistant to the Secretary of Defense. Over the next three years, he served as Senior Military Assistant to the Deputy Secretary of Defense and, briefly in 1979, as Executive Assistant to the Secretary of Energy.

In November 1980, President Carter lost his bid for reelection to Ronald Reagan, the Republican former governor of California. One of the reasons why Carter lost the election was criticism of his handling of a crisis in the Middle East.

In the fall of 1979, Muslim extremists in Iran had overthrown the ruling Shah, who was friendly to the United States. The United States embassy in the capital city of Teheran was captured. Many Americans who worked at the embassy were taken hostage and held for more than a year. President Carter ordered a dramatic rescue operation called Desert One, but it failed when helicopters broke down in the desert. It was a great embarrassment for the United States. The hostages were not released until January of 1981, just hours after Ronald Reagan took the oath of office as President. Some people have since charged that Reagan's representatives made a deal with the Iranian leaders to release the hostages after Reagan was elected in exchange for the promise to help Iran obtain arms. These charges, however, have not been proved.

The new president wanted to name his own staff and advisers, so it was time for Powell and his family to move again. He was promoted to brigadier general and named Deputy Commander at Fort Leavenworth, Kansas.

At Fort Leavenworth, he continued his hobby of fixing up old Volvos. He also liked to go jogging in the morning. As he ran, he often passed Buffalo Soldier Alley. He knew from his reading of military history that the alley's name honored the 10th Cavalry, one of several units of black troops who had fought in the Great Plains and Indian wars and helped settle the American West. He also knew that the 10th Cavalry had been based at Fort Leavenworth. It seemed to Powell that more ought to have been done to honor the Buffalo Soldiers at Fort Leavenworth than just naming an alley after them.

He read more about the Buffalo Soldiers and

Lt. Henry Ossian Flipper, a member of the 10th Cavalry, also known as the Buffalo Soldiers, was the first African-American to graduate from the U.S. Military Academy at West Point.

learned that Lieutenant Henry O. Flipper of the 10th Cavalry, in 1877, had been the first black graduate of the United States Military Academy at West Point, New York. He also learned that Lieutenant Flipper had been discharged from the Army because he was black. Flipper went back to civilian life and became a successful civil engineer, but he always felt bad about being forced out of the Army. Eighty years after it had discharged him, the Army reinstated him honorably, but by that time Lieutenant Flipper was dead.

Powell suggested to the top brass at Fort Leavenworth that a statue be erected in honor of the Buffalo Soldiers, but nothing much came of the idea at the time. Powell was soon called on to return to Washington, and there he had other things to attend to. In his absence, no one at Fort Leavenworth pursued the idea.

By 1983, Powell's old bosses, Caspar Weinberger and Frank Carlucci, had been named Secretary and Deputy Secretary of Defense, respectively, and they wanted him with them. He first served as an aide to Carlucci and then became Weinberger's top military aide.

By this time, the Middle East was the scene of many crises. Muslim extremists believed that friendship with Western nations had caused many Arab countries to forget their religious traditions. War broke out between Iraq and Iran, and in Lebanon between Muslim extremists and Muslim moderates. The fighting and terrorism spilled out into other areas of the world. In Italy, terrorists raided an airport and killed many innocent people. Terrorists hijacked a TWA airplane. They captured a cruise ship and killed an American man in a wheelchair.

Terrorists bombed a disco in Berlin where many American soldiers went to enjoy themselves. They bombed a U.S. Marine barracks in Beirut, Lebanon, killing 245 Marines. They put bombs in the cars of Westerners and took as hostages people from England and the United States.

The U.S. government seemed powerless to stop these random acts of terror. It was a very low time for Washington.

As Secretary of Defense Caspar Weinberger's senior military assistant, Powell soon came to be respected by everyone with whom he came into contact. People who wanted to get information to the Secretary believed that Powell was the one to relay it to him.

Powell's job was also to keep the White House and other departments of the government informed of all military operations. Just three months after he joined the Defense Secretary's staff, a major military operation occurred.

In October 1983, the United States invaded the small island of Grenada. The government of that island was afraid of an invasion from Cuba and asked the United States for protection. A combined United States force of Army, Marines, Navy, and Air Force swooped down on the island and made sure all the Americans there were safe and the government was secure.

Two Marines take a break during operations in Grenada.

Although the invasion of Grenada was popular in some quarters in the United States as well as in Great Britain, it was viewed negatively by the majority of Americans and other nations. United States forces found no Cuban troops to speak of, just some Cuban workmen. The deployment of United States troops from all branches of the military to such a tiny island seemed like overkill. Even though they faced little resistance, the United States forces found they could not communicate with each other — Army communication lines didn't connect up with those of the Marines, for example. It was not the moment of glory the

United States military needed to bring it out of the doldrums that had followed Vietnam.

In early 1986, the United States launched a military operation against the headquarters of Muammar el-Qaddafi of Libya. The United States believed that Qaddafi was supporting acts of terrorism against Americans in Europe and the Middle East. Qaddafi escaped harm in that raid, but after it he stopped working as openly against the United States. Powell played a major role in that operation, which was popular at home and in the rest of the world.

Powell played a minor role in another operation, this time one that was political, not military. It was a secret plan to sell weapons to Iran in exchange for the release of American hostages being held in Lebanon by terrorists with ties to Iran.

As the number of American hostages seized by Middle Eastern terrorists rose, some in the United States government decided to act on their own to get them released. Although the official policy was not to negotiate with terrorists, Rear Admiral John Poindexter, head of the National Security Council, his aide, Colonel Oliver North, and others began negotiating with Iran.

Iran was still fighting its war with Iraq and needed arms and other military equipment. Poindexter and the others offered to sell Iran arms. In return, Iran would not only pay for the arms but also would get the terrorists to release the hostages. The money paid for the arms would go into a secret fund to support the *contras*, a group that was fighting a civil war against the government of Nicaragua in Central America. The Reagan Adminstration supported the *contras* but could not get Congress to authorize any money to help them.

The plan to sell arms to Iran was illegal. So was the secret fund to support the *contras*.

The idea of selling arms to Iran had been suggested at the highest levels of government. Defense Secretary Caspar Weinberger had opposed it, and so had Colin Powell. But if they thought mere opposition would end the plan, they were wrong. Members of the National Security Council continued with it in secret. According to Weinberger,

Caspar W. Weinberger, former U.S. Secretary of Defense, who became close friends with Powell during Powell's assignment as a White House Fellow.

Powell "was the first one who started catching these very strange intelligence reports that made references to things we didn't know about. He brought them in to me, and I said I wanted to know a great deal more about it. He and I discussed it many times. When the final decision was made we saw it with the greatest possible reluctance and did what we were, in essence, ordered to do."

During the summer of 1985, Admiral Poindexter's National Security Council staff asked Colin Powell to furnish information about the availability and prices of TOW antitank missiles. Powell did as he was asked. That November, he was asked to coordinate an Israeli shipment of Hawk missiles to Iran, and he did so. President Reagan had not authorized this shipment, but Powell did not know that.

In January 1986, President Reagan authorized a second shipment of arms to Iran. Powell was the person who carried out those orders. But before he did, he wrote a memo to Admiral Poindexter. In it, he pointed out that by law Congress was supposed to be notified of any transfer of arms. Poindexter ignored the memo, and Powell did as he was ordered. He was relieved, however, when a few months later he was offered a position away from Washington. He had begun to feel uncomfortable there.

In June 1986, Powell was offered the command of the Fifth Corps, a force of 72,000 men stationed in Frankfurt, West Germany. Usually, that kind of command was given only to generals or lieutenant generals. But Powell's superiors felt he was the best man for the job. Along with the command came a temporary promotion to lieutenant general. Powell was glad to get the promotion, but he was even happier to have another military command. He and his family packed up and moved once again.

Powell had not been in West Germany long when a scandal erupted on the National Security Council. The secret plan to sell arms for hostages and then use the money earned to help the *contras* was exposed. President Reagan created a special commission, headed by Texas senator John Tower, to investigate the scandal. The Tower Commission held public hearings and ordered the main players in the plan to testify. They included Admiral Poindexter, Colonel North, and Robert McFarlane, the former National Security Adviser. Powell, reached in West Germany, was questioned by telephone and advised that he might be called to testify as well.

Colin and Alma Powell were barely settled in their new posting when he got another call from Washington. Acting on recommendations from the Tower Commission, President Reagan was reorganizing the National Security Council. Admiral Poindexter had resigned, and the President had named Frank Carlucci to succeed him as National Security Adviser. Carlucci wanted Powell to be his deputy.

*Lieutenant Colonel Oliver North responds to questions from the House Select Committee during the Iran-*contra *hearings, July 7, 1987.*

This time Powell said no. He told his friend that he was enjoying his new command and felt he had already spent too much of his career in Washington rather than out in the field as a soldier.

Powell once explained his feelings about commanding troops compared to serving in Washington by referring to military history: "There's an old expression, 'Better to be governor in the farthest province from Rome than to be number two in Rome.' It's great being a commander in the field, where you set your own agenda and are close to soldiers. That keeps you young. Nothing is quite as much fun as being a commander out where you're not trying to satisfy nine constituencies at once, where you're more insulated from the daily push and pull of Washington."

But Carlucci was not about to be easily put off. He called two more times. Two more times Powell said no. But after hanging up the third time, Powell felt concerned about the note of urgency in his friend's voice. He was beginning to have second thoughts. He called Carlucci back and told him that he'd been questioned about Iran-*contra* and the TOW missiles, and he might be called to testify. Carlucci assured him that he had already checked, and that Powell was "clean." Carlucci added, "I wouldn't ask you to give up this command if I didn't need you. The Commander in Chief needs you." Powell answered that if the President really wanted him, he would have to say yes.

Thus, when President Reagan personally called Powell to ask him to take the job, Powell agreed to do so. At a press conference in Washington, in January 1987, he explained his decision, saying, "I'm a serviceman, a soldier, and it looked like my service might be of greater use here."

4
National Security Adviser

The Powells packed up reluctantly. When they returned to Washington, it was about their eighteenth move, and this one was especially difficult because twenty-five-year-old Michael Powell, a lieutenant in the Army, was in West Germany. They had enjoyed being near him and did not like having to leave him so soon.

On their return, they found Washington in a tense mood. As the Iran-*contra* scandal unraveled in the course of weeks and weeks of testimony before Congressional committees, it became apparent that members of the Reagan Adminstration had broken the law by engaging in illegal activities. Colonel North and Admiral Poindexter were convicted of breaking the law, and Robert McFarlane tried to commit suicide.

Colin Powell was never called to testify publicly.

Instead, he appeared in private before various Congressional committees investigating the scandal. No charges were brought against him. Indeed, after the memo he had sent to Poindexter, pointing out that Congress was supposed to be informed of any arms transfers, came to light, he was regarded as a professional who had been following orders but who understood exactly what the law was. Powell was one of the few participants in the Iran-*contra* plan whose reputation did not suffer from the scandal. Even President Reagan's reputation was tarnished after it was learned that he had authorized the second arms transfer.

In the midst of Iran-*contra*, Colin and Alma Powell received terrible news from West Germany: Michael had been riding in a jeep when the driver lost control. The jeep had turned over, and Michael's pelvis was broken in six places. He needed twenty-two units of blood. He fought for his life for four days at the base hospital, and when the crisis had passed, he was flown to Walter Reed Army Medical Center in Washington, D.C., for surgery. Doctors feared that he would be confined to a wheelchair for the rest of his life because of the extensive nerve damage he had suffered. While Colin and Alma Powell feared the worst, they were careful not to show their fears to their son. Powell told Michael, "You'll make it. You want to make it, so you *will* make it!" A year and four months after the accident, Michael, though still walking with a cane, was well enough to marry his college sweetheart. He could not return to Army duty, so he got a job as a civilian employee in the office of the Secretary of Defense.

The Tower Commission, which had been created by President Reagan to investigate the Iran-*contra* scandal, had recommended many changes in the way the National Security Council operated. One of Powell's jobs was to make changes based on those recommendations. He did away with secret ways of operating and organized the National Security staff so that what had happened in Iran-*contra* would not happen again. He believed that the interagency process worked best when everyone had a chance to have a say in important matters, so that when a final recommendation was made to the President, all knew their views had been considered.

Powell won high praise for his work as Deputy to the Assistant to the President for National Security Affairs, Frank Carlucci. He had Carlucci's absolute trust. It was Carlucci's job to give the President a daily briefing. Often, Carlucci sent Powell in his place so that Powell and President Reagan would get to know each other better.

Powell and the President did get to know each other quite well. Ronald Reagan sometimes made insensitive remarks, causing some people to call him a racist. But Powell was able to be professional enough to overlook these remarks and to look for the things they had in common. The two joked about how they both had done poorly in school but had come very far in spite of that.

In November 1987, President Reagan named

Frank Carlucci, who later became U.S. Secretary of Defense.

Carlucci his new Secretary of Defense to succeed Caspar Weinberger. There was no question that Colin Powell should succeed Carlucci. When the President met with his advisers about whom to name to head the National Security Council, Powell's was the only name mentioned.

Powell was Reagan's sixth National Security Adviser. He was also a military man in a position that many people felt should be held only by a civilian, as Carlucci had been. Powell himself had once said he thought the position should be limited to civilians, to act as a balance to the military advisers. Powell felt he could advise the President in a fair manner and not be too biased toward the military.

Still, he made sure before he accepted the appointment that he could keep his Army commission. He still hoped one day to return to the field as a commander. In spite of the fact that Colin Powell was an Army man who wanted to keep his commission, there was no criticism of his appointment in Washington. In fact, more than one person remarked at how extraordinary it was that Powell had spent as much time in Washington as he had and apparently not made a single enemy.

The news media made much of the fact that Colin Powell was the first black National Security Adviser. Powell did not mind. Although he wished to be judged by his professionalism and his behavior, he was proud to be the first black in the office.

He made that clear in the public speeches he gave, including one at the Veterans Day luncheon for the auxiliary of the James Reese Europe Post, the oldest black American Legion post, in Washington, D.C. "Our history books seldom point out that 5,000 men, one sixth of the total of George Washington's army, were black, in the Revolutionary War," he said. He mentioned the 600 black men called up by General Andrew Jackson in the War of 1812 and the 186,000 black troops involved in the Civil War. He talked about how blacks had distinguished themselves in World War I and World War II, and how at last President Truman had signed an executive order outlawing segregation in the armed forces.

"When I came along in 1958, I was able to capture all of what was done before by men in segregated units, denied the opportunity to advance," said Powell.

"It's different now. We still have a long way to go. We should be grateful for what the men and women have done before. We cannot let the torch drop."

In January 1988, Powell gave a speech to a black Washington political organization, the Joint Center for Political Studies. In his speech, he remembered those who "suffered and sacrificed to create the conditions and set the stage for me." He also spoke out against continued discrimination, saying, "And I am also mindful that the struggle is not over . . . until every American is able to find his or her own place in our society, limited only by his or her own ability and his or her own dream."

When he made that comment, Colin Powell may have been thinking back to an incident that had happened to him the previous year, when, as Deputy National Security Adviser, he had been sent to a commuter airlines terminal in Washington, D.C., to meet an arriving official. The airline agent ignored him completely. Only after Powell identified himself did the attendant realize he had been ignoring a three-star general.

In his day-to-day work, Powell's race simply did not come up as a topic of conversation. He approached the job as a professional, and that is how he was treated in return.

One of his first big jobs was to coordinate the

December 1987 summit meeting between President Reagan and Soviet leader Mikhail Gorbachev, the first of seven international summits he co-ordinated between the two superpowers. That first meeting resulted in an important arms control agreement. At that meeting, for the first time, the Soviet Union agreed to mutual on-site inspection.

As head of the National Security Council, Powell often served as a spokesman for the Reagan Administration's military efforts. He argued on behalf of military and financial aid to the *contras* in Nicaragua. While members of Congress respected the way he made his arguments, they did not vote the funds requested.

Many Western hostages were still being held in the Middle East, and Powell spoke out against ever negotiating with terrorists. Eventually, however, he did agree to negotiation with a dictator — General Manuel Antonio Noriega of Panama.

Since early in this century, the United States has regarded Panama as strategic to its interests in the Western Hemisphere. President Theodore Roosevelt had persuaded Panama to sign a treaty to create a canal zone controlled by the United States, and the Panama Canal had been built across the country to aid United States shipping. Even after President Jimmy Carter agreed to give control of the canal back to Panama as of the year 2000, the United States wanted to keep Panama as a friend. Thus, the United States looked the other way as Noriega, a Panamanian army officer who had received United States training and who

General Manuel Antonio Noriega of Panama pictured here before his arrest.

became the country's leader in 1983, used corruption and fraud to tighten his grip on the small nation. The reason, say some, is that Noriega was providing the United States with valuable information on Cuba and other Latin American countries. To have his help, the United States turned a blind eye to his criminal activity.

After Noriega began supporting smugglers of drugs into the United States, however, he lost United States support.

In fact, he was under indictment by a United States federal court for his drug-smuggling activities. The State Department had the idea of offering him a deal: If he stepped down as leader of Panama, the United States would drop the federal indictment against him. Although Powell did not like offering deals to dictators, he was concerned that the alternative was to use American troops to overthrow Noriega. He was reluctant to use American troops to enforce United States drug laws. So, he agreed to the deal. The idea was dropped, however. A presidential election was coming up, and the Republican Party was concerned that any deal might hurt their chances of holding onto the presidency.

If President Ronald Reagan had been able to run for reelection to a third term, he probably would have retained Powell as his National Security Adviser because he was very pleased with Powell's performance in that job. But by law no president can serve more than two terms in a row. Ronald Reagan stepped down, but not before he had rewarded Powell with a fourth general's star.

Reagan's Vice President, George Bush, ran as the Republican presidential nominee against Governor Michael Dukakis of Massachusetts. Some Republicans suggested that he choose Powell as his running mate. This would have been an historic first, for no major party had ever backed a black candidate for the number-two spot on the ticket. Many other names were suggested to George Bush, who chose J. Danforth Quayle, a young senator from Indiana, as his running mate.

Powell had not discussed his own political party

affiliation in years. In 1963, he had sported an "All the Way with LBJ" bumper sticker on his car, but since he had been in Washington, he had decided it was best to keep his political views to himself. Still, he served as an informal adviser to Jesse Jackson in his campaign for the Democratic presidential nomination, which eventually went to Michael Dukakis. In November 1988, Vice President Bush won the election.

Before he was sworn in as President in January 1989, George Bush told Powell he wanted to name Brent Scowcroft as his National Security Adviser. On the day of the new president's inauguration, Powell left his White House office for the last time and went home to watch the ceremony on television. Then the telephone rang. It was the Army Chief of Staff, General Carl Vuono, calling to ask him to come back to active duty. Powell said he had not decided what he was going to do.

The telephone rang again. This time the caller was an agent from New York who said he wanted to represent Powell on the lecture circuit. Many organizations wanted him for speeches and special appearances. The agent said Powell could make as much as a million dollars a year just giving lectures. Powell told the agent also he had not yet decided what he was going to do.

He was at a crossroads in his life. He had served his nation well in both the capital and the field. He'd been in the Army for more than thirty years and was eligible to retire with a comfortable pension. He liked the idea of having time to spend with Alma, his daughter Linda, who wanted to be an actress, and his daughter Annemarie, who was then attending the College of William and Mary in Virginia, as her older brother and sister had. He was looking forward to the arrival of his first grandchild, who was due to be born soon to Michael and his wife. He also knew very well that his organizational abilities and his knowledge of the ins and outs of Washington would make him an attractive candidate for many high-level jobs in private business.

Sometime later, Powell took a piece of paper, drew a line down the middle, and titled the two columns "Reasons to Stay in the Army" and "Reasons to Leave the Army." He quickly filled the first column with reasons to stay. In the second column, the only reason he could think of to leave was "money." That was not enough reason to leave. Colin Powell called General Vuono back.

In April 1989, Colin and Alma Powell kissed their new grandson, Jeffrey, good-bye, and packed up for the move to Atlanta. Powell was scheduled to take over the United States Forces Command at Fort McPherson, Georgia. As head of Forces Command, he supervised all servicemen in the United States as well as the reserves and the National Guard. He was also responsible for assigning American troops around the world.

*General Colin Powell with his wife, Alma, at the installation
services where he was made head of the U.S. Forces Command
at Fort McPherson, Atlanta, Georgia, April 1989.*

But once again, he and Alma had just started to settle into their new life when they were interrupted. Four months after arriving in Atlanta, Powell took a call from President Bush. The President wanted to appoint him Chairman of the Joint Chiefs of Staff.

5
Chairman of the Joint Chiefs of Staff

The Joint Chiefs of Staff (JCS) was created in 1947, just after the end of World War II. It consisted of the four-star heads of the Army, Navy, Marines, and Air Force, and a Chairman. They meet in secret session every Monday, Wednesday, and Friday at two o'clock in the Pentagon in a tightly guarded room without windows, called the "tank." Not even the President of the United States knows what they talk about, but they have the power to set the military policies of the United States and to decide where the more than two million men and women in the United States armed forces are stationed throughout the world.

The Chairman of the Joint Chiefs of Staff has no legal position in the military chain of command, but his role is basically to command the armed forces on behalf of the President and the Secretary of Defense.

Since 1986, the Chairman of the Joint Chiefs of Staff, who serves a two-year term, has been the highest military official in the land. Before that time, he was merely the first among equals, with no more power than the other service leaders. In 1986, Congress passed a law making the Chairman of the JCS the principal military adviser to the President. Congress also gave the Chairman a Vice Chairman, a larger staff, and the authority to prepare strategic plans and the force structures of each of the services.

In appointing Colin Powell, President Bush passed over dozens of other senior military men — some with five stars — who were older than Powell and had served longer. In fact, at age fifty-two, Powell was the youngest Chairman ever to serve. He was also the only man to hold the job who had never attended the United States Military Academy at West Point or the United States Naval Academy at Annapolis, Maryland. In addition, chairmanship of the Joint Chiefs of Staff had previously followed an unofficial rotation pattern, so that the head of each branch of the military would have the chance to serve as Chairman. It was supposed to be the Air Force's turn to control the chairmanship. But Powell fit the bill where the President was concerned. He had many of the qualities the President admired. He was a team player, highly capable but modest, and he knew

General Colin Powell takes the oath of office given by Secretary of Defense Dick Cheney while his wife, Alma, holds the Bible, October 3, 1989.

how government worked from the inside. President Bush said at the press conference announcing his selection of Powell, "As we face the challenges of the nineties, it is most important that the Chairman of the Joint Chiefs of Staff be a person of breadth, judgment, experience, and total integrity. Colin Powell has all those qualities and more."

There was no public criticism of the appointment. No matter how some people felt about Powell's youth, his not having attended one of the military academies, or his not being in the Air Force, they had no personal criticism of Colin Powell. Indeed, he was almost unique in Washington because he had no enemies. Former Defense Secretary Caspar Weinberger said of Powell, "He has excelled in everything he has touched, and he always will. I don't think you can find anyone who has anything bad to say about Colin Powell, which is an extraordinary thing when you've been around Washington as long as he has — in highly sensitive and vital assignments."

What criticism there might have been may have been muted because he is black. On the other hand, there was quite a bit of public praise, because being the first black Chairman of the JCS was an important milestone. Overall, however, his color was not regarded as a major factor. As one former White House official put it, "No one ever thinks of Colin as being black, they think of him as being good."

It was a milestone he wished his parents had lived to see, but sadly they had died by that time. Luther and Maud Powell lived long enough, however, to see their son reach a level higher than they could ever have dreamed. And yet their dreams had been big enough to carry him along much further than he might otherwise have gone. Privately, Powell gave thanks for having such parents.

Publicly, he was modest about his appointment. He joked that the only drawback he could see about the job was that he and Alma would have to live in the graceful old house at Fort Myers, Virginia, that is reserved for the Chairman of the JCS. It sits at the top of a hill, with a view of the Washington skyline, and it is not the sort of place where he could have old Volvos lying around the yard. "It drags down the neighborhood," he said with a twinkle in his eye, referring to the fact that some whites don't want blacks to live in their neighborhoods.

Mindful of his roots, Colin chose *Ebony* magazine as the first publication to which he gave an interview after his appointment. "I've always tilted toward the black media," he explained. "I've made myself very accessible to the black press and I do that as a way of showing people, 'Hey, look at that dude. He came out of the South Bronx. If he got out, why can't I?'"

That Powell had good relations with the black press was also evident in the standing ovation he received when he spoke at the annual convention of the National Association of Black Journalists a few days after his appointment. Many in the room had not been fans of President Reagan, who had often been insensitive on racial matters. They had not supported the use of military force by the United States in Grenada and felt that blacks, who had served in disproportionate numbers in Vietnam and were overrepresented in the Army (more than thirty percent, with more than eleven percent officers, far higher than in any of the other services), should not be "cannon fodder" for the United States. But while Powell was a military man who had been closely associated with President Reagan, the black journalists still respected him greatly. They were proud that a black man had reached the level of achievement that Powell had.

General Powell chats with DeWayne Wickham, president of the National Association of Black Journalists, during the association's 14th annual convention, where Powell served as keynote speaker, August 17, 1989.

Once he became Chairman of the Joint Chiefs of Staff, plans for the monument to the Buffalo Soldiers that Powell had suggested be erected at Fort Leavenworth, Kansas, in the early 1980s, began to move along very quickly. Based on a painting by Lee Brubaker, called *Scout's Out*, it would be a more than life-size equestrian statue surrounded by pools and a waterfall. Ground was broken in July 1990, and Colin Powell attended the ceremony.

Powell found that there was little time for ceremonial duties, however. As he was being sworn in on the lawn of the Pentagon in early October 1989, a crisis occurred in Panama. A group in the

Panamanian military began to stage a coup against the dictator General Manuel Noriega. The leaders of the group appealed for American help, but Powell advised President Bush against giving it. He still didn't want to commit American soldiers to enforcing U.S. drug laws. But there was great pressure on the White House to intervene, and just hours later Powell authorized an attempt by American forces to capture Noriega. Unfortunately, it was too late. Noriega was rescued by soldiers who were loyal to him, and the Panamanian plotters were killed. A triumphant Noriega mocked the United States, which made Bush furious.

White House spokesmen explained that the United States had not trusted the plotters in the coup attempt and noted that Colin Powell and General Maxwell Thurman of the United States Southern Command based in Panama were too new to their jobs to be ready for such a major military action. But behind the scenes, the President gave the order for Powell and the Joint Chiefs to devise a plan for an invasion when the time was right.

Meanwhile, on December 1, another crisis occurred, this time in the Philippines. A military coup was attempted against President Corazon Aquino. With the approval of President Bush, Powell ordered United States forces stationed in the Philippines to help President Aquino fight off the coup attempt. Powell used just enough force to do the job but not so much that anyone would accuse the United States of unnecessarily interfering in Philippine affairs.

Given that cautious use of United States forces on foreign soil, it came as a surprise to many when the United States undertook a major invasion of Panama less than three weeks later. But some observers were not so surprised. They understood that President Bush had strong feelings against Noriega. While Bush had been head of the Central Intelligence Agency (CIA), Noriega had supplied the agency with information about drug smuggling in Central America. Now that it was clear that Noriega had at the same time been supporting the very illegal activities he had pretended to fight, Bush felt that he was a traitor.

Under the circumstances, the President needed little persuasion that an invasion of Panama was justified. Yet he felt there had to be a clear and compelling reason to order it.

It wasn't long before Panama gave the United States that reason. Three separate incidents challenged the United States to take action. A Marine officer was killed on December 19. An American couple was roughed up by Panamanian soldiers. Noriega's parliament declared United States-Panama relations in "a state of war." Bush wanted Noriega deposed. Powell recommended to the President that to accomplish that goal the United States launch a massive assault that could quickly take control of the country. The time for caution

General Powell briefs the media on the predawn invasion of Panama to oust General Manuel Antonio Noriega, December 20, 1989.

was over. If America was going to use force, then it should send in 26,000 soldiers, the forces necessary. Powell then put into effect the plan called Operation Just Cause, the name serving as a clear statement that the invasion of Panama was justified.

Powell decided if the United States felt it was really right to interfere in Panamanian affairs, then the United States ought to send in all the forces required to do what had to be done. The lessons of Vietnam came back to him. There was no point in going into Panama if they did not go in to win. He cautioned the President that it was unlikely they would be able to capture Noriega.

He also was concerned about putting the lives of so many United States troops in jeopardy. But he felt it had to be done.

Operation Just Cause was put into effect on December 20. Twenty-six thousand American troops were sent into Panama and quickly seized Noriega's headquarters, putting down all resistance from troops loyal to the Panamanian general. Noriega himself sought refuge in a Catholic church, but eventually he gave up and was brought to the United States to stand trial.

Operation Just Cause experienced problems, however. American troops broke into the offices of political parties that had supported Noriega and destroyed their records. United States troops also helped anti-Noriega Panamanian forces shut down newspapers and radio and television stations that had been associated with the dictator. Powell didn't believe the United States had any business interfering in those ways, and he called General Thurman and told him to put an end to such activities.

But aside from those problems, Powell was proud of Operation Just Cause. The United States invasion of Panama was the first decisive victory for American forces since World War II, and the majority of Americans supported the action. But there were also many Americans who did not believe the United States should have meddled in the affairs of a foreign country, or had "just cause" to invade Panama. They questioned why the United States had never released official figures of the number of Panamanians killed in the invasion, and there were scattered protests around the nation. City College had invited Powell to attend its 1990 graduation ceremony, in which the college planned to honor him as one of its most famous alumni. But after City College students, their faces painted white to symbolize civilians who died in the invasion, demonstrated against giving him the award, Powell declined the invitation. While he gave as his reason that he had other commitments, one suspects that he wished to avoid any unpleasantness.

Powell returned to his work on the Soviet-American arms control agreements. Things were proceeding quite smoothly, because for the first time since the end of World War II the United States and the Soviet Union were on friendly terms. With Mikhail Gorbachev as its leader, the Soviet Union was undergoing many reforms, including some freedom of the press, encouragement of private enterprise, and the opening up of trade with the West. Meanwhile, the countries of Eastern Europe that had been under Soviet domination since the end of the war were allowed to exercise more rights. In the space of a very brief period of time in the late 1980s, the wall dividing East and West Berlin was torn down; East Germany allowed its citizens to cross the "Iron Curtain" into West Germany and started reunification negotiations with West Germany; Romanian people overthrew their dictator, Nikolai Ceausescu; and Poland held free elections. The "Cold War" between the Soviet bloc

General Powell poses with Kristin Baker during her graduation from the U.S. Military Academy at West Point, where Baker served as brigade commander and the first female captain of the corp of cadets, June 1, 1990.

and the West, which had lasted more than forty years, was finally over.

In late 1989–early 1990, for the first time in many years, there were no wars being waged anywhere in the world. Some people dared to hope that war was gone from human life forever. But close observers of the Middle East knew that that area was a powder keg waiting to explode.

6
Operation Desert Storm

During the Iran-Iraq war, the United States had tried to remain neutral, although some in the government favored supporting President Saddam Hussein of Iraq as the lesser of two evils. Once the war ended with a cease-fire agreement, however, even many of Saddam's American supporters were concerned. In the course of the war, Saddam had built up large supplies of armaments and huge armies. Iraq was also developing chemical weapons that had been used against Iran at least once and that were used in great quantities to quell a revolt by the Kurds, a minority population within Iraq's borders. In the spring 1988 put-down of the Kurdish rebellion, 5,000 civilians died from mustard and hydrogen cyanide gasses, and possibly the nerve gas sarin, as well. Nations in the Middle East that were friendly to the United States, es-

President Saddam Hussein of Iraq, whose armed forces launched an attack against Kuwait and quickly gained control of that nation in August 1990.

pecially Kuwait, Israel, and Saudi Arabia, were worried about the huge military presence in their midst.

Perhaps the nation with the greatest fear of an Iraqi attack was tiny, oil-rich Kuwait on Iraq's southern border. So important did the United States consider Kuwait's oil reserves that in the summer of 1987 the United States had reflagged Kuwaiti oil tankers. Powell had supported that idea. He was concerned that Iran and Iraq, who at the time were still at war, might attack the tankers. He believed the tankers would be safer if they flew the United States flag. In that way, if either Iran or Iraq attacked one of the tankers, it would be an act of aggression against the United States.

Now Iran was no longer considered a military threat. But Iraq loomed as a dangerous neighbor of Kuwait's. Kuwait had more than enough oil to fuel Saddam's giant war machine, and after years of bitter war with Iran, Iraq needed both Kuwait's oil and its money. Rumors began to fly that Iraq might invade Kuwait.

Saudi Arabia was also fearful of an Iraqi invasion and asked the help of the United States in the event such an attack occurred. President Bush asked Colin Powell and Army general H. Norman Schwarzkopf to prepare a plan to use troops should a crisis arise in the Persian Gulf. They called the plan Operation Desert Shield because it was meant to be a force to defend Saudi Arabia, not an offensive campaign to attack Iraq. General Schwarzkopf was directed to assemble that defensive force as soon as possible.

Powell felt that any plan had to take into account the nature of the Middle East, so he started reading a history of the region. Explaining why he thought history was important, he compared it to a sporting contest: "I like to say, 'Guys, let's get into the stadium first before we play ball.' I always like to have a context for what I do, so I know I'm in the right stadium and I'm playing the right game. Then I can go on the field and play it. History helps put me in that context."

He wasn't sure, however, how helpful it would be in the case of the crisis in the Persian Gulf. "Frankly," Powell said in early October, "the only lesson that I can pull out of the history of the Middle East is that it'll never be uncomplicated and that history is not always the best judge of what's liable to happen in the future. These things in the Persian Gulf: For a number of years now we've had a certain balanced set of forces and balanced strategic interests. Now, it's all sort of up [in the air]."

What he meant was that for years, the United States would not have seriously considered publicly intervening in Middle Eastern affairs for fear of inviting a confrontation with the Soviet Union. Now, there was little chance that the two superpowers would disagree on Middle East policy. For years the United States had been reluctant to interfere in the Middle East because the Arab nations resented United States support for Israel and considered any interference an act of pro-Israel aggression. Now, Saudi Arabia and other Arab nations were more concerned about Iraq than they were about Israel. For the first time, the possibility actually existed that a multinational force might be willing to work together against Iraq if it invaded Kuwait.

Middle Eastern history also wasn't much good at giving clues about the behavior of Saddam Hussein, President of Iraq. Nor, for that matter, were all the U.S. intelligence reports about the man. He was known to have a huge ego and to show no mercy when he was crossed. He'd had close advisers shot when he suspected they might be against him. He had been cruel in putting down the Kurds. Some experts believed he was more talk than action; others believed he would never back down. American diplomats in the Middle East were said to have warned Saddam that if he attacked Kuwait, he risked retaliation from the United States. Apparently those warnings either were not strong enough, or Saddam did not pay enough attention to them. Saddam Hussein didn't think the United States would follow through on its threats if he went ahead with the invasion.

Early in the morning of August 2, 1990, 80,000 Iraqi troops crossed the border into Kuwait and quickly won control of the tiny nation. The rest of the world was nearly unanimous in its condem-

President Bush speaks before the Pentagon of Saddam Hussein's actions in Kuwait. Seated left, Defense Secretary Dick Cheney and right, General Powell.

nation of the invasion. The way was open for the United States to act.

Peaceful ways were tried first. The United States and other nations tried blockading Iraq's ports and levying sanctions against all trade with Iraq. All manner of high-level diplomacy was tried to bring about a nonviolent solution. Secretary of State James Baker was very successful in rallying support from many nations. The United Nations passed resolutions against Iraq and called for its withdrawal from Kuwait, although they were not unanimous. Several delegations, including China's, abstained or voted against the resolutions.

Meanwhile, President Bush had just about made up his mind to attack the Iraqi forces and free Kuwait. According to Bob Woodward, an editor at *The Washington Post* who later published a book about the Persian Gulf war entitled *The Commanders*, Colin Powell advised the President against rushing into an offensive military campaign. He suggested instead that the United States pursue a policy of containment and give sanctions an opportunity to work. When Bush did not change his mind, however, Powell began to plan the offensive strategy.

General Schwarzkopf was still in Saudi Arabia organizing a defensive force. When asked in early October if he could attack, he said he did not have the necessary troops or armaments, for more and more Iraqi troops had been sent into Kuwait, and they were massing along the Saudi border. Powell asked Schwarzkopf just what he would need to drive the Iraqi army out of Kuwait, and on October 21, he flew to Saudi Arabia to discuss plans with the general. The plan Powell presented to the President on October 30 called for a large-scale bombing campaign to begin in mid-January, to be followed by a ground war late in February.

The plan, called Operation Desert Storm, reflected the lessons Powell had learned from Vietnam. He realized that the American public was not patient, and so the armed forces should not let themselves in for a long, drawn-out war with no end in sight. He believed that once the decision had been made to go with force, that force should

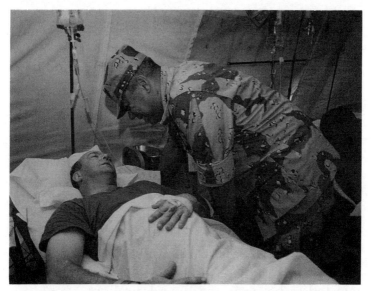

General Powell talks with an ailing soldier at the Air Transportable Hospital in Saudi Arabia.

be as massive and decisive as possible. In other words, go with everything you've got as fast as you can get it there.

The plan required almost doubling the 200,000 American forces in the Persian Gulf in a little more than three months. That meant a major call-up of the military reserves. Bush ordered that the plan be put into effect, and the largest military movement in history began. At the same time, he sent Secretary of State James Baker on a round-the-world tour to get support for a U.N. Security Council resolution authorizing the use of force. Everyone involved — the President, Defense Secretary Dick Cheney, Secretary of State James Baker, and Colin Powell — believed that the massive military buildup, combined with a U.N. resolution authorizing the use of force, might be enough to persuade Saddam to withdraw.

On November 29 the U.N. Security Council authorized the use of force if Saddam did not begin withdrawing his troops from Kuwait as of midnight Washington time, January 15, 1991. U.N. forces, commanded by General Schwarzkopf, began conducting practice amphibious attacks, which led Iraq to concentrate its forces mainly on fortifying Kuwait's border and coasts. Meanwhile, hundreds of thousands of American regular and reserve forces were transported to the Persian Gulf, along with sixty days' worth of food and supplies. Colin Powell and General Schwarzkopf wanted to be prepared for a long fight.

There was little question that U.S. air power was

General Powell and Defense Secretary Dick Cheney visit troops at a U.S. air base in Saudi Arabia, December 21, 1990.

up to the task of bombing Iraqi bases and supply depots. But there was some question about the ability of U.S. ground forces to succeed against Iraq's ground forces. Iraq's army was seasoned after the long war with Iran. U.S. troops were not accustomed to the desert, and its tanks and other machinery were not made for desert combat. Powell and General Schwarzkopf concentrated on drilling the troops so they would be ready for fighting in the desert. Hot and far from home, the regulars and reserves did their best to keep their spirits up as they waited to see what would happen.

Midnight, January 15, 1991, came and went, and Saddam did not signal that he would withdraw from Kuwait. President Bush gave the order to attack, and two days later, in the early hours of January 17, Operation Desert Storm began. For more than a month, United States and United Nations Special Forces flew bombing raids against Iraq's armed forces, bridges, and artillery. By the end of the air campaign, much of Iraq's air force had been grounded or destroyed, and most of its supply depots had been destroyed. However, much of the country was badly bombed, too.

Then, on February 24, ground forces moved in. United States troops aided by French, Egyptian, and Syrian forces attacked Kuwait to pin down Iraqis there. They made inroads into southeastern Iraq. In many areas, they found Iraqi soldiers who were much more willing to surrender than to fight, and they encountered little resistance. The biggest problem was the elite Iraqi Republican Guard forces, but even they were no match for the allies in Kuwait. On February 27, allied forces took Kuwait City, the country's capital, as well as the airport. By February 28, the war to rescue Kuwait was over, and it had been a stunning success.

No war is simple, however. After the cease-fire, Kurds and others in Iraq who were against Saddam Hussein revolted and expected support from the United States. But that support was not forthcoming. In spite of strong sentiment in the United States and elsewhere in the world, President Bush chose not to enter the civil war in Iraq on the side of the insurrectionists. As a result, millions of Kurds were forced to flee their homes and take refuge in Turkey and Iran. The refugee problem became so serious that at last the Bush Administration was forced to offer to set up refugee camps for the Kurds in northern Iraq. The United Nations, meanwhile, moved to create a buffer zone where the Kurdish refugees could be safe.

In spite of what many considered a moral failure on the part of the United States to support the Kurds, the victory in Kuwait was one that most Americans were proud of. The embarrassment of

General H. Norman Schwarzkopf and General Colin Powell smile at the crowds of Operation Welcome Home, New York City, June 10, 1991.

Vietnam had been put to rest at last. Plans were being made across the nation for celebrations to welcome the troops when they came home.

No two soldiers were more celebrated than Generals Powell and Schwarzkopf. In April, Congress authorized funds to have two special gold medals struck, one in honor of each man. Powell, who grew up in the Bronx, was invited to throw out the first ball for the New York Yankees' opening home game on April 15.

A potential pall on the limelight being cast on Powell was advance word about the Bob Woodward book, *The Commanders,* which was published in April and which reached bookstores in early May. Although he did not quote Powell directly, Woodward stated that privately Powell had expressed reservations about President Bush's desire to use offensive force against Iraq.

The idea that there had been dissension at the highest levels of government made headlines. Especially before the book became widely available, there was some speculation that the revelations in the Woodward book might lead to Powell's resignation as Chairman of the Joint Chiefs of Staff. But the book did not say that Powell had serious reservations about the President's strategy or that he tried repeatedly to change Bush's mind.

President Bush quickly took steps to quell any speculation that he was unhappy with his Chairman of the JCS. Referring to his position as Commander in Chief of the Armed Forces, Bush noted on May 2 that the Chairman "owes the Commander in Chief his advice. When the Commander in Chief makes a decision, he salutes and marches to the order of the Commander in Chief. And if there's anybody that has the integrity and honor to tell a President what he feels, it's Colin Powell."

To make sure everyone understood that he continued to stand by Powell, the President reappointed him to a second two-year term as Chairman of the Joint Chiefs of Staff on May 23 — four months early.

At the news conference where the announcement was made, reporters still had questions about the Woodward book and on how much the President and the General had disagreed over United States strategy against Iraq. "We were together throughout this exercise," said Powell, "and efforts to suggest that there was distance between the President and his advisers are incorrect." With that news conference, the matter was essentially put to rest.

Colin Powell returned to his duties as Chairman of the JCS, taking time out to be an honored guest, with General Schwarzkopf and Secretary of Defense Dick Cheney, at two huge celebrations in honor of the troops who participated in Operation Desert Storm. The first was in Washington, D.C., on June 7, and the second, on June 10, was a traditional New York City ticker tape parade.

While Colin Powell appreciated all the attention,

Thousands revel in the festivities of the Operation Welcome Home ticker tape parade, New York City, June 10, 1991.

he was not overwhelmed by it. He understood that Americans have a short attention span and that it would not be long before they turned their thoughts to other things, especially the many problems that faced American society, such as the economy, drugs, and crime.

Some people suggested that the United States ought to take the will and skill it had used to drive Saddam Hussein's forces out of Kuwait and use them to attack the problems at home. The drug war might be won if the military services launched an operation against drug smugglers.

This was not a new idea, and Colin Powell had thought about it. While before the Panama invasion he had rejected the idea of using the armed forces to enforce United States drug laws, he now accepted the idea of using those forces at least to seal the United States borders against drug smugglers. "We're losing too many young Americans, particularly African-Americans, to drugs," he once explained. "I'm devastated over what's happening in the inner cities. There's nothing America has to do of a higher priority to its security — national security and all kinds of security — than to get a handle on this drug problem."

He still felt it would be risky, however, and he was against using military personnel to make drug arrests. It was a very politically sensitive issue, and one that would require legislation by Congress.

But what *was* to be done about the problems of

poverty, homelessness, and nondrug-related crime that affected all Americans, but especially African-Americans? Couldn't the United States marshall its resources to attack those problems, too? Powell believed that might be possible, but he did not see the military playing much of a role in that kind of war. He did, however, believe that he could help in a small way by serving as an example to young people, black and white, but especially black. In spite of the great demands on his time, and the many speaking invitations he received from august bodies of influential people, he accepted as many invitations as he could to speak to young African-Americans.

Powell told them there was no substitute for hard work and study, and that as blacks more would be expected of them. But he also told them, "Don't let your blackness, your minority status, be a problem to you. Let it be a problem to somebody else. You can't change it. Don't have a chip on your shoulder, and don't think everybody is staring at you because you're black. It may be true, but let that be their problem, not yours."

On the day he threw out the first ball for the Yankees' home opener (unfortunately, the team lost to the Chicago White Sox), Colin Powell also visited his old neighborhood. "I remember, I remember," he mused as he rode along the avenues and streets along which he had raced his bicycle as a youngster. At Morris High School, he recalled the front door, the auditorium, the park where he

General Colin Powell receives a standing ovation from the students of his alma mater, Morris High School, in the Bronx, New York, during homecoming ceremonies.

had practiced with the track team. He also remembered, he told the students of Morris High School, "the feeling that you can't make it. But you can," he said. "Stick with it. I'm giving you an order. Stick with it."

Glossary

Military Units

Battalion: a unit composed of a headquarters and two or more companies, batteries, or similar units

Brigade: a unit consisting of a variable number of battalions

Company: a unit, as of infantry, consisting usually of a headquarters and two or more platoons

Division: a tactical unit composed of a headquarters and usually three to five brigades

Infantry: soldiers trained, armed, and equipped to fight on foot

Platoon: a subdivision of a company, usually consisting of two or more squads

Regiment: a unit consisting of a number of battalions

Squad: the smallest unit, usually designated as a rank or a line in formation

Second Lieutenant
First Lieutenant
Captain
Major
Lieutenant Colonel
Colonel
Brigadier General — one star
Major General — two stars
Lieutenant General — three stars
General — four stars
General of the Army — five stars

Bibliography

Adelman, Ken. "What I've Learned," *The Washingtonian*, May 1990, pp. 67+.

Barnes, Fred. "Powell in Command," *The New Republic*, May 30, 1988, pp. 14–16.

Barry, John, and Evan Thomas. "A Second Look at the War," *Newsweek*, January 7, 1991, p. 18.

Booker, Simeon. "Colin L. Powell: Black General at the Summit of U.S. Power," *Ebony*, July 1988, pp. 136–138+.

Breslin, Jimmy. "Bronx Lot Holds America's Dream," *Newsday*, March 3, 1991, p. 3.

Brown, Marshall. "Powell Reaches the Pinnacle of Pentagon Power," *Black Enterprise*, October 1989, p. 22.

Clift, Eleanor, and Thomas DeFrank. "Bush's General: Maximum Force," *Newsweek*, September 3, 1990, pp. 36–38.

"Colin Powell Named First Black and Youngest Chair of Joint Chiefs of Staff," *Jet*, August 28, 1989, pp. 5–7.

Current Biography, Vol. 49, No. 6, June 1988. Bronx, NY: H.W. Wilson Company, 1988, pp. 46–49.

DeFrank, Thomas. " 'The Ultimate No. 2' for NSC," *Newsweek*, November 16, 1987, p. 63.

Friedman, Saul. "Four-Star Warrior," *Long Island Newsday*, February 11, 1990, pp. 10+.

Friedman, Thomas, and Patrick E. Tyler. "From the First, U.S. Resolve to Fight," *The New York Times*, March 3, 1991, pp. 1+.

"General Colin L. Powell, Chairman of the Joint Chiefs of Staff," official biographical notes.

"Gen. Colin Powell Awarded State Dept.'s Top Honor," *Jet*, October 17, 1988, p. 5.

"Gen. Colin Powell Cites Black Military Legacy at D.C. Veteran's Day Affair," *Jet*, November 30, 1987, p. 18.

"Gen. Colin Powell's Advice to Young Blacks Today: Prepare and Be Ready," *Jet*, September 11, 1989, pp. 12–15.

MacKenzie, Richard. "Pulled to the Top by His Bootstraps," *Profiles*, October 8, 1990, pp. 8+.

Manning, Steven. "The U.S. Invasion of Panama," *Scholastic Update*, February 9, 1990, pp. 8–11.

Nelan, Bruce W. "Ready for Action," *Time*, November 12, 1990, pp. 26–31.

Powell, Colin L., "American Foreign Policy: Opportunities and Challenges," *Department of State Bulletin*, October 1988, pp. 51–53.

_____., "Economics and National Security, East-West Relations," *Vital Speeches of the Day*, January 15, 1989, pp. 194–197.

_____., "U.S. Foreign Policy in a Changing World, Keeping Democracy Alive," *Vital Speeches of the Day*, May 1, 1990, pp. 418–421.

Randolph, Laura B. "The World's Most Powerful Soldier," *Ebony*, February 1990, pp. 136–142.

Range, Peter Ross. "Powell Brings Peace to Policy War Zone," *U.S. News & World Report*, April 25, 1988, p. 35.

Rowan, Carl T. "Called to Service: The Colin Powell Story," *Reader's Digest*, December 1989, pp. 121–126.

Seaman, Barrett. "A 'Complete Soldier' Makes It," *Time*, August 21, 1989, p. 24.

Tyler, Patrick E. "Bush Reappoints Gen. Powell to Top Military Post," *The New York Times*, May 24, 1991, p. 1.

Weinberger, Caspar W. "General Colin Powell — An Inside View," *Forbes*, January 22, 1990, p. 31.

Wolff, Craig. "Gen. Powell Returns to the Bronx, and Remembers," *The New York Times*, April 16, 1991, pp. 1+.

Woodward, Bob. *The Commanders*. New York: Simon & Schuster, 1991.

Index

Page references in italics indicate material in photographs.

About the Author

JIM HASKINS is a professor of English at the University of Florida at Gainesville, and lives in New York City and Gainesville, Florida. He is the author of over eighty nonfiction books for young readers, including *Black Dance in America: A History Through Its People*, which was a Coretta Scott King Award Honor Book for Nonfiction; *Black Music in America*, which won the Carter G. Woodson Award; and *Scott Joplin: The Man Who Made Ragtime*, winner of the ASCAP Deems Taylor Award. He also wrote *Christopher Columbus: Admiral of the Ocean Sea; The Day Martin Luther King, Jr., Was Shot;* and *The Sixties Reader.*